The Flawed Journ

THE FLAWED JOURNEY OF A HEART

First edition. October 12, 2024.

ISBN: 979-8227207043

Written by ikram miah.

Hi,

This book is about my journey, the ups and downs, and the vast array of emotions I felt in moments past.

I hope this book and these words can help you in whichever way you need, may it be to heal or may it be to escape. I hope you may find solace in my words.

Thank you.

This is dedicated to all those who have loved.

Content

The winds allow me to feel the essence of your embrace.
The rain allows me to feel the subtleties of your touch.
The sun allows me to feel the warmth of your radiance.
The world allows me to still feel you.

Only You

Doesn't matter if it's in this life or another.
I'd still choose you.

If I could give you one thing,
It would be the ability to see yourself through my eyes.
Only then you'd see how beautiful you truly are.

Souls

We may have just met.
Yet somehow it's as if our souls were bonded many lifetimes before.

The Aura that Fills my Heart

The missing pieces of my heart belong to you.
Your essence, your aura, you.
You complete me.

Art

You're art.
It's not how you look.
It's how you make me feel.

The pain of losing you is something I've learned to cherish.
It reminds me of how I loved & felt in a time so pleasant.
The pain is simply memories of us, of you.
Thank you.

It's never "Right person, wrong time".
Because when you meet the right one.
Time loses meaning.

Heaven in Your Embrace

The essence of you was the only heaven I'd ever known.
The warmth of your embrace still hugs me on the colder days.
How could I ever forget you?

What is love?

I ask myself; "What is love?"
Love is not just a feeling, love is not just a state of mind.
Love is also work.
Sometimes the feeling of love comes and goes.
What you do in between these highs and lows makes love what it is.
You must try to hold on to this love for as long as you can.
That's why love is hard, but that's why love is worth it.
That's love.

Waves

You're like the heavy waves crashing onto the shore of the beach without remorse.
You come so powerfully to leave your mark and disappear suddenly.
You've left your mark on me.
You've damaged me in a way I thought was impossible.
I'm broken and you didn't care enough.

Shadows of Your Touch

Time stood still when I met you.
I felt an everlasting embrace shining upon me, you fulfilled me.
You're gone now & that's fine...
I'm not fine, I miss you.
I miss your touch, your scent, your smile.
I miss the little things that made you.
All I'm left with now is the ghost of you.
I'm stuck – in every shadow, I feel you.
Haunting me, hurting me.

Letting Go of Holding On

They say "Good things come and go".
Is that why you keep going?
I've tried to hold you close.
To weave your essence into the fabric of my days but,
There's no more use in trying.
For my heart has learned the dance of letting go.
I've made peace with the silence of your absence,
Each empty hour is a canvas painted with bittersweet memories,
Where laughter once bloomed like wildflowers,
Now shall rest in stillness.

Forever With You

I feel like time is never wasted with you.
We could sit in silence forever and with you, I'd still feel joy.
With you, everything feels right.

I Love You Most

I want to love you when you're low,
When you think there's nothing more.
I want to hold you ever close, and tell you...
I love you most.

Seasons

You're the 4 seasons in a year;
You're spring, summer, autumn, and winter all in one.
You're the joy & freshness of spring.
The warmth & radiance of summer.
The glee & coziness of autumn.
The beauty & elegance of winter.
Without you the seasons are meaningless, you're the essence of it all.

Perfections of Your Imperfection

I want to love every crack in your mirror,
Every tear in your eyes,
Every freckle on your shoulders,
Every wrinkle on your face.
I want to love you broken, I want to love you flawed.

Once Ours

It's better to have loved & lost
Than to never have loved at all.
At least we shared our light, our stars, our sky.
Go be happy, spread your wings and fly.

Drifted

Although our worlds have drifted apart,
I had you once.
That's enough for me.

The Rain

The rain washes away the pain.

It's the mark for redemption and recovery, washing away the bad and the good.

It's a sign to restart & rebuild.

This is the beauty of rain, the start of recovery.

As raindrops ripple onto our skin and our clothes, it reminds us to let go and move forward.

That is rain.

Haunted Blessing

My heart crumbled into a million pieces from just a few words.
Tears volcanically erupted from my eyes endlessly & effortlessly.
I sat in silence, in pain and heartache.
You gave me something I never thought I'd have.
Happiness.
Yet here I am, sitting in a painful silence trying to forget you.
You'll forever haunt me.

Space

I close my eyes & let my mind go astray.
I close my mind & go to space.
I close my eyes, I'm freely floating.
I close my mind, time has no meaning.
I'm all alone here in space.
The silence here is peaceful.
I open my eyes to this crowded place.
I'm hurting, it's lethal.

Maybe in another life, we worked.
A 6-word story.

You

In every other possible universe...
I'd still choose you.

I Can't Forget

I can't forget the way you made me feel.
I can't forget the way you laughed, and smiled.
I can't forget your touch.
I can't forget you.

A Lifetime in Seconds

Maybe time running out is a gift.

I'd give you every second I can find because every second with you is worth a lifetime.

I don't hate you.
I don't hate how sad you made me feel.
I don't hate how much you broke my heart.
I'm not angry either, I thought I'd be – but I'm not.
I can't find any reason to hate you.
Maybe in those shattering moments of utter heartbreak, I was angry, but only with myself.
I let me down.
You cross my mind a lot & even if the memories bring me pain, they don't bring hate.
They bring an ambivalence into my heart... in a good way.
They remind me of the way I felt.
I'm glad you came into my life, you showed me what it is to love.

My Face, Your eyes

Your needs are my needs.
You're my face, I'm your eyes.
You complete me.

When Love Sets Free

I loved you enough to let you go.
I couldn't hold onto someone slipping away, even if it killed me inside.
I still do care about you more than you'd ever know.
But letting you go was the only right thing to do.
I'm okay with it.
Go blossom into the beautiful rose you're meant to be.

Stars & Skies

Finally, the stars & the blue skies
Don't make me think of you any more.
It was a journey and a half for sure,
It was sad you couldn't love me any more.
The way I did, and cradled your thoughts.
The way I'd move mountains for you and more.
But now those same stars & skies
Don't remind me of you any more.

Still

I still remember your favourite colour, favourite number, and birthday.
I still remember how you'd get shy when I'd compliment you.
I still remember our endless conversations and our joyful laughter.
I still remember you.

The Moon Knows Your Name

I used to talk to you, now I talk to the moon.
I tell the moon all about you.
How you looked, how you spoke, how you smiled.
The moon is all I have to remember you by.
It's bittersweet how we share the same moon.
How the moon still sees you, while my heart is crying in your absence.
I wouldn't change it for the world for I still talk to the moon.
About you.

Sleeping to See You Again

Conversations with my ceiling,
They're forever never ending.
We always talk about you,
And the little things you'd do.
Like how you used to smile,
Then get bored for a while.
Now all I can do is sleep just to meet you,
To remember all the little things you'd do.
For the conversations with my ceiling are always...
About you.

I'm Trying...

We've lost touch, we've let go...
At least I'm trying to.
We said bye, we're no more...
What can I do?
You're gone now, I'm broken...
I'm hurting.
You're gone now, I'm letting go...
I'm trying.

Die to Grow

Sometimes... we have to die a little bit each time.

We have to accept that dying inside is a chance to learn.

We have to be able to withstand the pain of the past versions leaving us.

This can leave us feeling a little emptier each time but...

That's just life, right?

Every part of us that dies, is a part of us that was unable to bear the burden of living in such a constant state of hurt.

Every part of us that dies is a chance for another part to grow, to blossom.

This life is filled with its various ups and downs.

We just have to die a little to carry on marching forward.

To be better.

And to be better, we must die a little bit each time.

Live For You

The greatest things in life happen unexpectedly.
They happen spontaneously.
They happen when you're just living your life.
Live your life doing what's best for you, what makes you happy.
The universe is receptive, it will give back... in due time.
You won't necessarily get what you want but what you deserve.
Continue living this life as best as you can.
Lead with a clean, honest, and good heart.
What's meant for you will come your way, endure the trials & tribulations.
Just keep going, I promise you, things will be better.

Every Phase of the Moon

Let me love you like the moon.
Through every phase; full, half, or barely visible.
Let me love you every time you feel happy, sad, or miserable.
On the days you feel like honey or you feel blue,
I want to be the one who holds you together like superglue.
So let me love you like the moon.
Every phase you go through I'll be there side by side,
With you.

Purpose

Look around you and tell me... what truly has no purpose?
Do the stars not have a purpose? Does the rain not have a purpose?
They do.
The stars light up the beautiful night sky, the rain replenishes the plants.
So tell me, do you not have a purpose?
You do.
It might not feel like it at times but you really do matter.

Heartbroken in June,
My heart broken by you,
Left drowning in the oceans of deep blue.
Scathed by your daunting tunes,
On Sunday afternoons.
The scent of your harrowing perfume,
Open the wounds I tried so hard to close.
Lingering on my clothes,
The smell still in my nose.
Your ghost still floats throwing its hooks and blows,
My soul... left with the burden of June.
Because losing you was losing me too.

Our Books

In the book of you,
I was merely a chapter.
Yet you are my whole book.

Never My Forever

You weren't meant to be my forever,
Neither was I yours.
Our time together was a fleeting moment,
A glimpse of what could have been.
We danced in the shadows,
But never in the light.
We held each other close,
But always at arm's length.
We tried to make it work,
But knew it wasn't meant to be.
So here we stand, at the end of us,
Knowing that our love was never meant to last.

Roads of Reluctant Return

All the roads lead to you,
Every turn, every detour.
Even the ones I took to forget you.

You asked, "Do you love me?"
I didn't reply.
For not even words know how to describe you.

You Before Me

We were never... us,
We were always you then me.
In the effort of loving you,
I was losing me.
But letting you go let me be free.
No longer lost in the shadows of you,
Finally, I'm me.

The Invisible String Theory

When two people are meant to be,
They are connected by an invisible string.
No matter the time, place, or situation.
They will find each other over and over and over again.
This string may stretch or tangle but will never break.
This string allows two souls to be bonded,
For lifetimes before and lifetimes after.
So worry not.
This string will always lead the two souls to each other.

Rose Gold Reveries

If you can't sleep at night,
Know that you're awake in my dreams.
Still dancing in the rain on that rose gold summer night.
In each other's arms, fearless of the world around us.
Know that in my dreams,
we're still us.

When Love Becomes a Burden

Maybe it was me taking away your sadness.
Maybe it was you bringing me darkness.
We were stuck in the depths of misery,
Left wondering if you're missing me.
The day we tore apart was the day I fell apart,
The missing part of me was left with the broken parts of you.
Left you feeling free from the aches of the blue.
Loving you was like oxygen for me, a part of me.
Knowing you can't love me back became an addiction,
For loving you was like breathing to me.

Stronger

Stop living in the past, you'll be depressed.
Stop living in the future, you'll be anxious.
Live in the present, and take each step as it comes.
Life doesn't get easier.
You get stronger.

Isn't it Easier Being Cold?

Isn't it easier being cold?
All the nights I spent in pain.
The only one to listen was my ceiling.
Words couldn't understand my hurt.
The sky grew darker,
The rain got heavier.
My soul cried and cried,
My mind fought so many battles.
So tell me...
Isn't it easier being cold?

Amongst the Common, A Masterpiece

You are a star in the galaxy of forever.
You are a blade of grass in the garden of life.
Standing amongst the ordinary,
Yet standing apart.
A singular soul,
A work of art.

We Were Till We Weren't

How we'd watch us grow
How we'd Ebb & flow
How I watched you glow
In the winter's snow.
How I loved you so
How we are no more
Now I reap and sow
My broken heart and soul.

The Sun & Moon

Every night the sun gives himself up so the moon can have her stars.
Every star is a part of the sun, for the moon to be a little less lonely.
Time keeps them apart yet love knows no bounds.
How the sun still gives the moon what he can regardless of the time or distance.
The way the sun misses the moon is the way I miss you.
Every day I'll miss you,
Every day I'll care.

Goodbye

4 am and the birds are whistling.
The sun slowly rising.
My phone silent,
Yet my mind still screaming.
No one to hear my cry,
No one to see my hurt.
Drifting into the abyss of endless despair.
Hopeless. Helpless.
My eyes slowly closing.
Darkness arising and my pain, fading.
Peace arriving and my soul, evading.
I think I'll keep my eyes shut for a while.
Goodbye.

Forgetting to Forget You

I have held many hands yet still my palms feel empty,
None of them fill the spaces quite like yours did.
Constantly gasping for air, breathless.
My hollow lungs yearn for the oxygen you were for me.
Mindlessly replaying the harrowing tunes of your laughter over and over
again,
Forgetting to forget you.
I wish to lay my head on your lap,
Knowing that it is now impossible.
I would find you in total darkness,
You mute and I deaf.
The only place I can now find you is when I close my eyes,
Only then can I breathe and only then can I hear.

An Angel in the Rain

As raindrops ripple on your velvety skin.
Standing in the middle of an ocean of elegance,
All I see in an angel,
Blessed with heavenly eloquence.
Everything you do is magic,
Everything you touch glows.
How ever did I find you?
I guess only God knows.

Eyes Like Morning Sun

I never believed in love until I met you.

Now, I understand how cliché that is but I mean it.

I knew love was a thing before but it was until you happened when I truly believed it.

It's every time I see those eyes,

Every time I hear your voice,

Every time I feel your touch, my soul feels at ease.

You are like the morning sunlight glistening upon me with your warmth

You are the reason I believe in love.

My Reality

I don't see you in the stars and the skies,
That's what dreamers do,
I see your reflection in my eyes,
In everything I do,
Because you and only you,
Are my reality.

Everything I Am

I can't promise you the world.
Neither can I promise you the moon and the stars.
But... I can promise you everything I have.
Everything I can.
Everything I am.

Till Then, I'll Live

And surely one day I too will leave,
Simply a memory,
A whisper in the wind.
But for now, I guess I'll live.

Silence Speaks Your Name

Not even words know how to describe you.

How could it be?
Always at arm's length
But never tried to reach.
Always in front of one another
But didn't want to see.
Until... we did.
With you, I found my peace,
My happiness, my ease.
But all good things must come to an end
With that so did the book of you and me.
Find your happiness, I'll wait.
Like you say,
"If it's written" then it will be.

The Beauty of Imperfect Love

Nothing in this life is perfect.

These words are riddles with honest imperfections.

But with each and every word, I will try to show to you

My honest and pure love.

Behind every word, every sentence is each and every ounce of Love I can give to you.

Behind every flaw and every crack I'll stand.

Endlessly waiting for you.

Endlessly loving you.

When Words Fall Short

I had ran out of words to speak for you
So instead I learnt how to write.
In ink, I found a voice, an easeful embrace,
A whisper that glimmers where heartbeats collide,
Each phrase a confession, where secrets abide,
Crafted in twilight, draped in angelic grace.
The pulse of your name flows through every line,
Your laughter, beaming in-between each word.
So whilst the words fell short,
My soul learnt to write.

Beauty in the Broken

Not everything in life is meant to be beautiful.
Yes, you can find the beauty in it but,
Understand to take bad and learn to change,
Learn to grow and embrace the pain.
Not every tear is weakness, nor every scar, defeat.
They're stitches in life's canvas, your journey, incomplete.
In this patchwork existence, continue to march and strive
Weave your tapestry, stitched tight with your fight.
Yes, beauty is a choice, but so is the pain,
But know, in every crack, the light pours in just the same.

Dreams in Sunbeams

Loving you is like loving the sun.
I love you knowing I can never reach you,
A mirage of dreams trapped in golden hues.
Yet still, I adore you – my ungraspable love.
My eternal glow, from the skies above.

Love from Afar

I love you in my mind, knowing I'd never get hurt,
I love you from afar, knowing I can never get burnt.
I love you in whispers that daylight can't mend,
In shadows where dreams and silence blend.
My fingers grasping ghosts of a touch I long for,
Every heartbeat a secret.
From a distance, I'll forever paint you with brushstrokes of grace.
A place behind your shadow,
A place I know no pain can grow.

The Spaces You Fill

Each whisper of you fills the air like perfume.
Your laughter dances, dispelling the gloom.
My older memories envy you,
For you have somehow taken up all the space in my mind.
Your essence, a tide, that ebbs and then flows,
In currents of moments, where each memory glows.
I search for the shadows where quietness grows,
Yet you paint every corner, like spring after snow.

A Simple Soul

A simple soul,
Just another heartbeat in the room.
Never one to truly stand out.
Yet, she too has a story,
Full of highs and lows.
Her wisdom exceeds the grasp of words,
Her eyes have seen many things,
Yet her heart has felt more.
She speaks softly, but her words roar.
A simple soul,
A beautiful soul.

Lies Behind Those Eyes

When I realised
That your lies hide behind
Your real eyes
How could I?
How could I not see the signs
That behind your smile lines
Were the white lies
Hidden in plain sight.

A Glimpse of Paradise

An angel in disguise,
Lingering beneath the stars and the skies.
Insatiable to my eyes,
Stupendous I can't deny.
How can one not look twice?
An angel from paradise.

Me Before You

I miss the me before you,
The way I was.
But no matter what I do,
I can never be free from the ghost of you.

My Mother

My mother, such a beautiful soul.
I hope every tear you've shed is simply a river made for you in heaven.
Your laughter – the harmonies of paradise.
Your smile – a gift from God.
I hope to find even a glimpse of the love you have given me.
Thank you mum,
I love you.

The Storm Between Us

Your love is like thunder thudding against my chest,
Warmth of lightning I cannot rest.
Is it bad I love you like the west?
But don't have the faith of the east.
We can't meet or stay together and feast,
For my love, a raging beast.
I cannot have you or that's what I think at least.

- HK

Mindlessly Waiting

Leaves grow, tears flow
More and more.
It's quarter to 4,
And you still haven't made it back to my door.
I rest against it,
Waiting mindlessly whilst my head taps it.
Where are you?
This part is you cue,
The part where you come back to me,
The part where our feeling come to meet,
I miss you my darling, my rose, so sweet.

- HK

Not Loud Enough

I finally realized she meant everything to me but
I meant nothing to her.
I can't seem to exist loud enough for her to listen,
And I've been living in a delusion that she loves me
As much as I'm forced to love her.
Let her sleep with a heavy heart
And overthink for days.
Let her sleep thinking she's not good enough
Even though I laid it out on the line.
Let her sleep yearning
For a love my heart already gave her.
Let her sleep knowing I put her first,
She didn't care enough to know it.
I wish my heart could accept what my mind already knows,
That the love we once had
Died a long time ago.

- HK

Thank you for reading along this journey with me, here's to many more chapters in our storied adventures.

Ikram.

Thank you to all who have accompanied me on my journey, and a special thanks to my brother for the use of his poems.

9 798227 207043